The Illustrated Story of President Heber J. Grant
Great Leaders of The Church of Jesus Christ
of Latter-day Saints

Copyright © 1982 by
Eagle Systems International
P.O. Box 508
Provo, Utah 84603

ISBN: 0-938762-07-9
Library of Congress Catalog Card No.: 82-70686

First Printing May 1982

First Edition

Lithographed in U.S.A.
by
COMMUNITY PRESS, INC.

A Member of
The American Bookseller's Association
New York, New York

The Illustrated Story of President

HEBER J. GRANT

Great Leaders of The Church of Jesus Christ of Latter-day Saints

AUTHOR
Lucille Reading

ILLUSTRATOR
B. Keith Christensen

DIRECTOR AND CORRELATOR
Lael J. Woodbury

ADVISORS AND EDITORS
Paul & Millie Cheesman
Mark Ray Davis
L. Norman Egan
Annette Hullinger
Beatrice W. Friel

PUBLISHER
Steven R. Shallenberger

A
Biography Of
HEBER J. GRANT

Heber Jeddy Grant was the seventh President of The Church of Jesus Christ of Latter-day Saints. He was born in Salt Lake City, Utah, on November 22, 1856, to Jedediah M. and Rachel Ivins Grant. When Heber was only nine days old, his father died, leaving Heber and his mother nearly penniless. Out of this difficult beginning Heber developed strong faith and a great desire to share and help others in need.

As Heber grew, he nurtured a powerful determination to develop many skills and to prove himself successful in them. As a boy, he persistently developed baseball, penmanship, and other skills he valued.

At age nineteen, Heber was called to serve in the presidency of the first Young Men's Improvement Association of the Church. In 1877 Heber, then twenty-one, married Lucy Stringham. Three years later he was called by President John Taylor to act as secretary to the general superintendency of the MIA.

In 1880, when only twenty-four years of age, he was called to be President of the Tooele Utah Stake. He was the youngest stake president in the Church at that time. Just two years later, in October, 1882, President Grant was called to be a member of the Council of the Twelve. Elder Grant initially questioned his worthiness to stand as an apostle, especially at such a young age. But through prayer he received a sure witness that he was indeed worthy to serve and that this calling was intended for him. Fifteen years after being ordained an apostle, Elder Grant became a member of the general superintendency of the YMMIA. At this same time he was also appointed business manager of the newly founded *Improvement Era*.

In 1901, Elder Grant was called to open and preside over a mission in Japan, where he dedicated the Japanese Islands for the preaching of the gospel. After returning from Japan in 1903, he presided over the British and European Missions until his release in 1906.

After the death of Joseph F. Smith in 1918, Elder Grant, age sixty-two, was sustained as President of The Church of Jesus Christ of Latter-day Saints. He served twenty-seven years as President, longer than any other man with the exception of Brigham Young.

President Heber J. Grant dedicated the first temples built in the twentieth century. He dedicated the Hawaii Temple in 1919; four years later, in 1923, the Alberta Temple; and then in 1927 the Arizona Temple.

Heber J. Grant was President of the Church during the Great Depression that began in 1929. To help the Saints through these economically hard times, President Grant instituted in 1936 the Church security plan, which later became the present Church welfare program. As well as being a great spiritual leader, President Grant was a wise businessman and, in spite of the depression, was able to establish the Church on a firm financial base.

Heber J. Grant was a faithful leader. He taught the Saints through both deed and word that "we are the architects of our own lives, not only of our lives here, but the lives to come in the eternity. No commandment was ever given to us but that God has given us the power to keep that commandment." Heber J. Grant lived a life of great service to others and constantly worked fully to comply with all of the commandments.

President Heber J. Grant died on May 14, 1945, in Salt Lake City at the age of eighty-nine.

Snow lay deep over the Salt Lake Valley. When the children became tired of playing in it, they would sometimes wait for a sleigh to come by so they might "catch a ride" on its runners.

The most beautiful sleigh in all the valley was one owned by Brigham Young. Nearly every afternoon he would go for a ride while his driver guided a fine team of horses over the frozen ground.

As six-year-old Heber watched this sleigh, he noticed how far its runners stuck out behind the rest of the carriage. "What a perfect place on which to stand and ride," he may have thought. One day he ran out when the sleigh slowed down and took hold of the back of it. "I'll only ride a block or two," he probably thought. "Then I'll jump off." It was exciting to ride through the crisp air as the horses tossed their heads and the sleigh bells tinkled merrily.

The horses ran swiftly through the town and beyond it into the country, not slackening their speed at all. The bitter wind and snow swirled around him. Heber gasped breathlessly, watching the steam rise from his open lips that were numb with cold.

"Please help me to get back home safely," he prayed, his teeth chattering. "Oh, and what will President Young do if he finds me riding on the runners of his beautiful sleigh," he mused in anticipation and then shivered with fear.

When the horses had gone more than five miles, they came to a frozen stream and slowed down at last to make their way across it. "Now is my chance," Heber said to himself as he jumped off and began running toward his home.

But President Brigham Young turned, saw Heber, and called to his driver, "Stop! Stop! That little boy is nearly frozen. Put him under the buffalo robe and get him warm."

The cold and frightened runner-rider snuggled thankfully under the warm robe. Soon Heber heard a kind voice ask, "What is your name, boy?"

"Heber Jeddy Grant," the boy whispered.

"Why you must be the son of Jedediah Grant!" President Young exclaimed. "I knew him well. He was my counselor at the time you were born. Now, Heber," he went on, "you must tell your mother that I want her to send you to my office in six months. I want to have a good visit with you."

"From that time," Heber reported many years later, "I was intimately acquainted with President Young until the day of his death."

11

Heber was born in Salt Lake City, Utah, on November 22, 1856, to Jedediah M. and Rachel Ivins Grant, both of whom had known sorrow and endured hardships as they crossed the plains with the Mormon pioneers. Jedediah had been elected to be the first mayor of Salt Lake City. His first wife and a little daughter died during the trek west. Jedediah was lonely and, after reaching "the valley," married Rachel. When Heber was born, his father said, "Rachel, he is so tiny. I must take good care of both you and Heber." He was so anxious to take care of her and their new son that he kept getting up at night to attend their needs. It was bitterly cold during these nights and Jedediah took a severe chill that turned into pneumonia. He died when Heber was just nine days old.

Rachel was left almost penniless at the death of her husband. In order to support herself and her young son, she did sewing for others, took in boarders, and did any other work she could to earn a little money. She had much difficulty financially, and Heber often heard her pray for help. "So near the Lord she would get in her prayers," he remembered, "that they were a wonderful source of inspiration to me from childhood to manhood."

Sometimes, however, she grieved because she could not supply the little family with needed clothes. One Christmas she cried, "Oh, I haven't enough money to buy Heber even a stick of candy. What kind of Christmas can he possibly have?" And sadly she watched Heber put on his thin coat that she knew could not keep him warm. The next year as November approached, she understood when he said, "Mother, all I want for my birthday is a nice warm coat."

"I'll see what I can do, Heber," she nodded thoughtfully.

A few weeks later as Heber was hurrying on an errand, he saw a boy just his size who was crying with cold. The boy was wearing a thin sweater and Heber shivered, remembering how it felt to be cold. As he hurried by, the crying boy looked at Heber's new, warm coat with such longing that almost before he knew what he was doing, Heber stopped, took off the coat, and handed it to the boy. "Here," he said, "you must wear this coat. I have another at home."

That very afternoon Heber's mother saw him wearing his old thin coat instead of the warm birthday one. "Heber," she asked in amazement, "what have you done with your lovely new overcoat?"

For a moment he wondered how he could tell her he had given it away. After a few moments of silence he finally explained, "Oh, Mother, I saw a boy who needed my coat lots more than I do, so I gave it to him."

"Couldn't you have given him your old coat?" she asked.

Heber longed to have his mother understand. He looked up anxiously into her face and saw her eyes were misted with tears. Then he threw his arms around her as she answered her own question. "Of course, you couldn't, Heber," she said softly. "Of course, you couldn't."

This generous spirit of sharing was an outstanding quality of Heber J. Grant throughout his life. His love for others and his great desire to help them were evident to many, especially to needy widows. Both before and after he became President of the Church, he, like the Savior, "went about doing good." (Acts 10:38)

"Will you please tell me how much you are owing on your home," he wrote to one widow, "and let me join with you fifty-fifty in paying it at once instead of paying it by the month?"

Another time he wrote to a woman who was having some financial problems: "Dear Sister, I am happy indeed that I have been able to be of some little assistance to you. Is your home all paid for? If not, please let me know how much still remains."

THINK ABOUT IT:

1. How did Heber's mother teach him about the power of prayer?
2. Tell how Heber, as a boy, learned to share work with his mother.
3. Did Heber J. Grant love to share with others? How do you know?

When Heber was a boy, he was determined to become a good baseball player. He was tall and lean but not very strong. In his neighborhood there were three baseball teams. He was put on the one with the youngest and the poorest players, while all of the other boys who were Heber's age were players on the first team. "You're playing on the little kids' team," the others would tease him. "You're a sissy." This hurt Heber, but he just kept right on practicing with them and praying that somehow he could make the best team in the neighborhood.

He earned money shining the boots of the boarders in his mother's home to buy a baseball. Then he asked his neighbor, Bishop Woolley, "May I throw my ball against your adobe barn?"

"I suppose that would be fine with me, Heber," the bishop responded.

Heber threw and caught the ball until it sometimes seemed that the barn gable would be pounded in. Watching him, Bishop Woolley would just shake his head and walk away, murmuring, "What a waste of time. That Heber is surely the laziest boy in the whole Thirteenth Ward."

Often Heber's arm ached so badly that he could not sleep nights. "Where does it hurt, Heber?" his mother would ask softly and then apply cold compresses to ease the pain.

Before the summer was over, Heber's arm grew strong. His throwing, catching, and batting were also good. "Why don't you come and play baseball with us?" a friend his own age asked. "We're the best team in the neighborhood," another chimed in. "We could sure use your strong throwing arm." "When do we play?" Heber asked. He was elated. Later, to his great joy, he became a member of the "Red Stockings" baseball team that won the championship of the entire Utah Territory. And he was acclaimed as one of the team's best players!

That which we
persist in doing
becomes easy to do;
not that the nature
of the thing has changed,
but that our power
to do has increased.

Heber showed this same baseball determination when playing marbles, learning to sing, and improving his penmanship. At first his writing lacked grace and style. Many described it as "chicken scratches." But he wanted to improve his penmanship so that it would represent him well. He decided to practice writing regularly, and he did so for many years. Eventually he so developed this skill that he won first place in penmanship at the Utah Territorial Fair. Later he even taught penmanship at the University of Deseret (now the University of Utah).

This ability to accomplish successfully so many tasks was well-expressed for him by a quotation from Ralph Waldo Emerson: "That which we persist in doing becomes easier for us to do—not that the nature of the thing has changed, but that our power to do has increased." Heber often cited this quotation and lived by its principles.

Once, hearing an appeal for tithing, Heber offered fifty dollars that the bishop knew he had just earned. The bishop returned forty-five dollars to Heber, saying: "Five dollars is your fair share." But Heber offered all the money again and said: "Bishop Woolley, didn't you preach here today that the Lord would reward four-fold? My mother is a widow and she needs two hundred dollars."

The bishop replied: "My boy, do you believe that if I take this money, you will get your two hundred dollars quicker?"

"Certainly," responded Heber.

Bishop Woolley took the entire fifty dollars. Afterwards Heber suddenly thought of a way to earn $218.50 through a business transaction. The following day he paid $21.85 in tithing, making him just $3.35 short of the $200 he needed for his mother.

Heber always lived faithfully and preached that "We are the architects of our own lives, not only of our lives here, but the lives to come in the eternity. No commandment was ever given to us but that God has given us the power to keep that commandment."

When he was only nineteen, Heber was called to serve in the presidency of the first Young Men's Improvement Association in the Church. Five years later, in 1880, he was called by President John Taylor to act as secretary to the general superintendency of the MIA.

Shortly after this Heber was called to be the President of the Tooele Utah Stake. In his first talk to the stake he said, "I will ask no man in Tooele to be a more honest tithe payer than I will be; I will ask no man to give more of his means in proportion to what he has than I will give; I will ask no man to live the Word of Wisdom better than I live it; and I will give the best that is in me for the benefit of the people in this stake of Zion."

Heber J. Grant served longer as President of The Church of Jesus Christ of Latter-day Saints than any man excepting Brigham Young. When Joseph F. Smith, who was president just before Elder Grant, learned that he was near death, he asked for Heber. "He must come and see me. There is something I must tell him." Heber came promptly, and as he knelt by the bedside of the dying prophet, President Smith whispered to him: "The Lord bless you, my boy. He is greater than any man. He knows who he wants to lead his Church, and he will bless you."

Early in Heber J. Grant's presidency, he dedicated the first temples built in the twentieth century. Their appearance differed from that of the nineteenth century Utah temples. Local or regional architectural themes, such as American Indian or Polynesian motifs, were worked into their designs, proclaiming that The Church of Jesus Christ of Latter-day Saints is a Church for all countries and peoples—not only for Utah or America. As a prophet of the Lord, he dedicated the Hawaii Temple in 1919. He dedicated the Alberta Temple in 1923 and the Arizona Temple in 1927.

In 1929 America was stricken by a great and terrible depression. Money was so scarce that some people were nearly starving. Sometimes after lining up to get aid from charities or from what were called "soup kitchens," they received only a bowl of soup and one or two pieces of bread. Often even highly skilled workers, such as craftsmen, artists, and business executives, found that no one wanted to hire them. "I'm eager to work—even for pennies. But jobs are so few that I can't even get enough to eat," a worker complained. Often those who did work were paid much less than they had earned before the Great Depression began.

"We've got to give and accept help from each other. We've got to organize and care for ourselves," said some of the Saints.

And so in 1926 President Grant introduced the Church security plan, which later became the present Church welfare program.

It was often said of President Grant: "Through all the twenty-seven years that he has been President of this Church, Heber J. Grant has been not only a great spiritual leader, but an exceptionally wise businessman. I don't know anyone so talented in financial management."

He led the Church through some extremely hard times. Because of his understanding of sound economics, he was able to direct the affairs of the Church in such a way that, in spite of the Great Depression, the Church was established on a firm financial basis.

Under the leadership of President Grant, the welfare plan continued to help people, and additional Church programs were planned and expanded. Among these were the Tabernacle Choir broadcasts, which were started in the early days of radio (1922). Because of President Grant's wise decision to show what Latter-day Saints were really like, the world began to have better feelings toward the Church.

THINK ABOUT IT:

1. What did President Grant teach Church members to do during times of hunger and poverty?
2. How did he teach the world that Latter-day Saints are good and honorable people?

At one time a man was writing a biography of President Grant. This man asked of Heber, "Have you a message to give to boys and girls, one that would still bless their lives after you are dead?"

"Indeed I have," President Grant replied. "Tell them to try to make others happy and to aid them in carrying their burdens in life. Then they will be sure of happiness, not only in their lives here, but in the life to come. Tell them to always be punctual, truthful, and virtuous."

Heber J. Grant died on May 15, 1945. An editorial written at that time summed up the life of this loving man and great leader: "God fashioned him in heart and mind and body, in ability, in experience, and in wisdom."